FROM NOBODY TO BESTSELLING AUTHOR!

How to Write, Publish & Market Your Book

Naresh Vissa

Naresh Vissa

FROM NOBODY TO BESTSELLING AUTHOR!

How to Write, Publish & Market Your Book

ISBN-13: 9781724084170 (Krish Publishing)
ISBN-10: 1724084178
ASIN: B07HQ3MBMY

Table of Contents

ABOUT THE AUTHOR

Naresh Vissa is the author of the #1 bestsellers FIFTY SHADES OF MARKETING: Whip Your Business Into Shape & Dominate Your Competition and PODCASTNOMICS: The Book Of Podcasting... To Make You Millions. He also self-published – through his book publishing company, Krish Publishing – TRUMPBOOK: How Digital Liberals Silenced a Nation into Making America Hate Again and The New PR: 21st Century Public Relations Strategies & Resources to Reach Millions. He has helped multiple authors write, publish, and market their bestselling books.

Vissa is also the Founder & CEO of Krish Media & Marketing – a full service online and digital media and marketing consultancy and agency. He has worked with leading publishers, media firms and institutions such as CNN Radio, JP Morgan Chase, EverBank, The Institute for Energy Research, Houston Rockets, Houston Astros, the American Junior Golf Association, Agora Publishing, and Stansberry Research.

Vissa graduated Magna Cum Laude from Syracuse University's Honors Program with degrees in broadcast journalism, finance and accounting. He earned a Master's Degree from Duke University's Fuqua School of Business.

USA Today, Yahoo!, Bloomberg, MSNBC, *Huffington Post*, Businessweek, *MSN Money*, *Business Insider*, *India Today*, *Hindustan Times* and other domestic and international media outlets have featured Vissa.

Subscribe to Naresh Vissa's free mailing list at www.nareshvissa.com.

You can contact Naresh Vissa at Naresh at KrishMediaMarketing dot com.

FROM NOBODY TO BESTSELLING AUTHOR!

How to Write, Publish & Market Your Book

Dedication
THE SECRET TO FANTASTIC WRITING

This will probably be the longest dedication you'll ever read… because you're reading a *book*… that *I wrote*. It's a miracle that this is in your hands. Here's why…

To be an author, you need to be able to write… a lot. Writing is not easy. And it has to be fluid and engaging. Some of the most educated people I know (with Ivy League graduate degrees) are astonishingly crappy writers.

I'm a good writer… because my Amazon and Goodreads reviews (and sales) say so… and my friends and enemies say the same.

I'm a two-time, #1 bestselling author. I've written for USA TODAY, *Business Insider*, *MSN Money*, and been syndicated on all sorts of networks.

How did I get good at the written word?

Writing legends say that the best way to write well is to read a lot. That's partly true, but not entirely…

As a kid, I didn't read anything outside of the *Sports* section of the HOUSTON CHRONICLE. Reading was my worst subject in grade school. I used to read those lame *American Girl* books for my required reading tests because they were short and easy to get through. If it were possible to fail the Reading section of the SAT, I would've failed.

And I wasn't a good writer as a child either. I'm still traumatize by my 1st grade writing teacher Ms. Bevans crumpling up my creative writing stories and throwing them in the trashcan multiple times in front of the rest of the class, yelling at me for plagiarizing the most boring, irrelevant literature, or just being a downright illiterate.

But although I sucked at reading and writing, I aced my grammar tests. And fortunately, I was taught *real, actual* grammar in elementary and middle school.

Once I got to high school, I was able to take my English grammar knowledge and apply it to a foreign language – French. *Learning French* for nearly seven years helped me understand English language mechanics (like passive voice, split infinitives and reflexive pronouns) better.

If you understand the fundamentals of grammar and sentence structure, then the sky is the limit to become a good writer. You can learn to become a good reader later (which I did during college). You can learn how to add voice and style to your writing (which I did in my mid-20's after going through copywriting training).

But learning the basics of the written word or language is something that can only be acquired at a very early age.

So, this book is dedicated to the teachers in Houston who taught me a bunch about grammar and the fundamentals of language… the diagramming, marking up sentences, and memorizing the linking verb and preposition songs were all worth it.

Ms. Allison Sliva, Ms. Marilyn Melton, Ms. Lisa Herman, Ms. Mary Hall, Ms. Sandy Flint, Ms. Kristi Winston from The Village School (where I went to elementary and middle school)…

My French teachers Ms. Rita Michael (also from The Village School) and Ms. Jane Murdock from The Kinkaid School (where I attended high school)…

I'm sorry I haven't kept in touch with most of you. I'll make sure you all get free copies of this book.

Thank you.

Your student forever,

Naresh Vissa

INTRODUCTION

Every good writer needs inspiration, and in my case, I've been (un)fortunate to live a life of constant frustration. Rather than choose to react to such frustrations in emotional ways, I made the decision early in my life that I wanted to be a writer – even if nobody read my work. I told high school and college classmates about book ideas I had. The only problem was: I never actually *wrote* or *got started* on any of these projects.

I've always had an interest in writing. After serving as my high school newspaper's Sports Editor, I attended one of the leading journalism schools in the country at Syracuse University and gained enough notoriety with my print and broadcast reporting that I was given my own business column (which ended up being syndicated for a few months) for the school's flagship newspaper, *The Daily Orange.*

Then, the fire was lit under me…

Many years ago, before Amazon took over self-publishing, I was in therapy dealing with an issue, and my counselor told me that I had three choices:

1) Keep seeing her and complaining about the same shit. Eventually, she predicted she would not want to respond to my appointment requ-ests.

2) Keep thoughts to myself, and mindfu*k myself all day with no solutions or ability to move forward to the present.

3) Write out all my problems and issues and then try to concoct solutions – no matter how unfeasible they were – as if I were publishing for the world to read in the *New York Times* or for purchase at Barnes & Noble.

Option 3 changed my career – and my life – forever. The timing of my realization happened to coincide with the rise of self-publishing platforms for authors, as well as my fledgling interest in online and digital publishing, marketing and e-commerce.

My first #1 bestselling book, <u>PODCASTNOMICS: The Book of Podcasting… To Make You Millions,</u> was a result of my irritations with leads or clientele for my company, Krish Media & Marketing. We had folks on a weekly basis either 1) asking us what podcasting was, or 2) using us as consultants for their own podcasts but not listening to or executing anything we'd coach them on. With 1, I kept answering the same questions over and over again and got tired of leads wasting our time for no money. With 2, I'd find myself yelling at the walls or constantly shaking my head out of annoyance.

So, I decided to answer all the questions I kept on responding to over phone or e-mail… through a book, which ended up selling more than 10,000 copies and has brought in hundreds of thousands of dollars worth of business through sales, projects, coaching / consulting, and speaking engagements. For $4-7, anyone around the world now has access to my knowledge and expertise on podcasting – through <u>PODCASTNOMICS</u>. This is a lot cheaper than the hundreds of dollars we charge for a few hours of coaching, or thousands of dollars we charge per project.

Surprisingly, the discounted book has only *helped* my business and me – not hurt it. The number of people who bought the book, read it, and then reached out for additional coaching and consultation far surpassed the number of people who became paying clients *before* the book came out.

The success of <u>PODCASTNOMICS</u> inspired me to write my next #1 bestselling book… this time, a primer on online and digital business and marketing: <u>FIFTY SHADES OF MARKETING: Whip Your Business Into Shape & Dominate Your Competition</u>. Like <u>PODCASTNOMICS</u>, <u>FIFTY SHADES OF MARKETING</u> was the result of constant frustration with my clientele and other folks who just didn't see the online and digital marketplace… and also like <u>PODCASTNOMICS</u>, <u>FIFTY SHADES OF MARKETING</u> got me all sorts of speaking opportunities, new clients, and consulting.

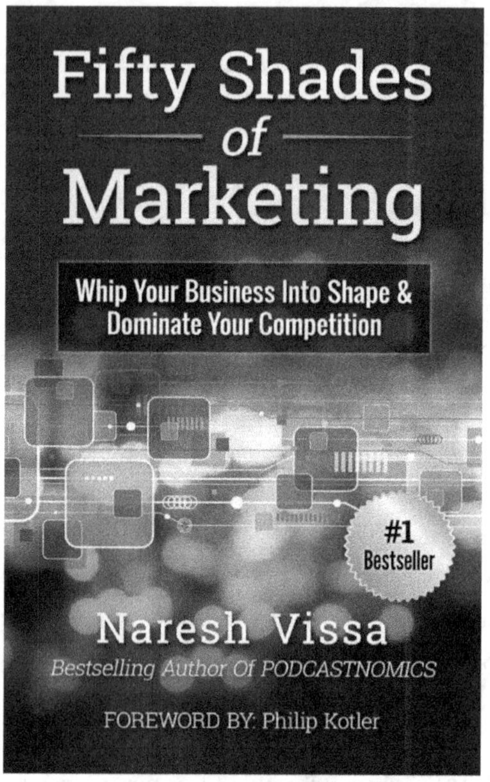

I've since gone on to write or publish a few more books — not just mine, but other authors' / clients' as well — some of which have reached #1 on several Amazon categories or sold incredibly well. I frequently give lectures or do media interviews on book publishing, and my spinoff business, Krish Publishing, has never been stronger.

I hope you will take some value away from this book. I'd love to hear your feedback via a review on Amazon or you can reach me directly at Naresh at

KrishMediaMarketing dot com.

Is self-publishing bad?

When I first heard about self-publishing, I thought it was an amateur sham. As years passed by, I recognized that many of the books I'd read were self-published. I then went through my mini-library and realized I had no idea who the publishers were of 100% of my books.

That's when it hit me: if I wrote a great book with an awesome cover design and no formatting, spelling or grammatical errors, then it doesn't matter to anyone whom the publisher is.

With self-publishing, I get to write whatever I want. My voice can be heard, even if nobody can hear it. Not one person can say "No!" to me. I hate it when people say "No!" to me. It's a mental problem I have. But thank you Amazon and self-publishing for your solution to my problem!

If you want to become an author, then self-publish your books on Amazon, BarnesAndNoble.com, iTunes, Audible, etc. This book you are reading will help you do that. That's what Fifty Shades of Grey author E.L. James did. She's sold more than 200 million copies of her books and generated more than $5 billion of franchise sales (books, movies, merchandise, paraphernalia, speaking gigs, etc.).

The only day is now. There are no more excuses.

The world as we know it is improving day-by-day. Processes are becoming more efficient, and the cream is finding quicker, newer ways to rise to the top of the crop.

Don't be left behind.

Chapter 1
4 REASONS WHY PUBLISHING A BOOK WILL MARKET YOU FOREVER

Books are still the fundamental building blocks to education. When we're little, our parents and teachers *make* us read. As we get older, the reading becomes copious thanks to textbooks.

Here's what writing a book can do for you:

1. Branding

People still judge books by their front covers, so seeing your name and book on major platforms like Amazon, iTunes and iBooks builds enormous credibility. People may not buy or read the book, but they will forever place you positively and authoritatively.

Over the long haul, this is great for your brand. You can leverage your brand to get you more business through speaking, consulting, new business opportunities, and more.

2. Establishes You As A Thought Leader

Books carry knowledge, and knowledge gives us power. So, the people who write books not only have knowledge, but perception views them as powerful figures… not just in their field, but also in society as a whole. Noble authors command a lot of respect from the public because of the emphasis on education worldwide.

3. Lead-Generation

Outside of becoming a powerful and respectable authority figure, authors can funnel in readers as leads to their businesses. If you offer something of value to anyone, they will reciprocate and give you value back. It's one of the unwritten laws of human nature and karma.

4. Pass-Along Effect

The greatness of books is that they don't disappear. Some of the great classics we read in high school have survived over the course of centuries. So even if your book doesn't receive good reviews or sell any copies today, it can still become a hit 20 or 200 years down the road. If you're alive to see this, great. If not, then your lineage can reap the benefits… or, if you leave a business behind, then it can benefit.

Chapter 2
THE DEATH OF TRADITIONAL BOOK PUBLISHING

Traditional publishers are not as effective as they used to be. They are stuck in the 20th century ways of conducting business. They don't understand the 21st century, New PR. They offer services that anyone can now emulate.

Worst of all, they have a minimum length requirement of about 250, double-spaced Microsoft Word pages. Why is this length so stringent? Because 250 pages will ensure the book will be thick enough for text to print on the *spines* of hardback and paperback books at bookstores. If your book can't meet this requirement, then traditional publishers won't even read your book title.

The only problem with a 250-page, fundamental requirement of traditional publishers is that bookstores are dying. Borders went bankrupt. ***The Guardian* reports that Barnes & Noble is closing stores by the month. And this is largely because:**

> **a.** It's easier for people to shop online on Amazon instead of visiting a physical store. *Forbes* reports that 65% of new book sales (both print books and e-books) are bought on Amazon. This number is increasing each year while physical bookstores are going out of business.

b. Self-publishing has allowed authors to publish directly to large online marketplaces.

To put it another way: the spines of books are now irrelevant, which means the length of any published book is now negligible.

There is no minimum length to *self-published* books. There are people – like Kamal Ravikant – who have written small books a little over 5,000 words and sold tens of thousands of copies.

A traditional publisher prides themselves on two things:

1) They can give you an advance (which is going down every year)
2) They can get you in bookstores (which are disappearing).

For that, they take 85% of your sales. What a rip-off!

The death of traditional book publishing opens up limitless opportunities for self-published books and authors. *Bowker* found that nearly a million books were self-published in 2017. Smashwords reports that independent books now compose more than 20% of the book market. That means one out of five books available today have been self-published. That's incredible considering that traditionally published books go all the way back to Gutenberg's printing press in 1455. Self-publishing hit the radar around 2007. *Forbes* reports that 2008 was the first time in history that more books were self-published than those published traditionally.

There are two main reasons for the death of traditional publishing:

1) **Choice** – Because of self-publishing, there are now so many books out there – too many, really – and this means that consumers have more options to find content that fits their needs and interests. With traditional book publishing, a fixed number of books are published every year, and this limits the amount of content they're able to pump out.

2) **Price** – Self-published authors have control over the pricing of their books. Most of them offer consumer-friendly pricing. Smashwords reports that indie titles retail at an average price of $2.99 to $3.99 while traditionally published books retail between $7.99 and $14.99. That's a 55-75% discount and pricing advantage that indie authors have over traditional publishers. Readers are clearly factoring price into their purchasing decisions and opting for high-quality, lower-priced titles over the more expensive, traditionally published books. Self-published authors can also offer their Kindle e-books for free or 99 cents. Traditional publishers wouldn't even think about running such campaigns because it cheapens their

brands and earnings potential. Free and discounted promotions are incredibly powerful discovery techniques for my books. I couldn't have sold more than 11,000 copies without such dynamic pricing.

Nevertheless, a lot of work is required to write and self-publish a book. It can take years for someone to do it themselves or tens of thousands of dollars to outsource it all (including the writing).

The rest of the book goes through how you can do it all yourself… without breaking the bank.

Chapter 3
HOW TO PICK AN IDEA, TOPIC OR THEME FOR YOUR BOOK

The first element of a successful book is writing on a particular subject with a clear focus and expertise. The narrower the topic, the better.

The book you're currently reading, for example, is all about book publishing… how to ideate, write, publish and market a book completely on your own, step-by-step.

That's niche. You know, as a reader, what to expect when you read the subtitle or buy my book.

As a writer, you must have the knowledge to discuss a topic in-depth. It should be something that you are passionate about or are screaming to say. In other words, writers should write books because they have something they *have* to say. It's tough for other people to emulate emotion or passion.

Many times, I write because I know I have strong, convincing arguments and points on certain subjects, but my friends and family won't listen to me because they aren't interested or are too busy with their lives. They don't want to hear me ramble about book publishing or digital marketing.

So my solution is to write a book for myself. The people who are interested will come later and follow. If the book is good, then they will find your stuff.

Avoid Trends

Don't waste your time trying to become a hack author – someone who writes about random topics just because they're trending on Amazon, Google Trends or Twitter. It's impossible to be an expert in disjointed subject areas, and if you're just writing because you think you'll sell many copies, then you'll quickly be labeled as a fraud whose writing isn't genuine.

Businesses *must* take into account every trend and disruption into their operational strategy… because people start businesses with the intention of generating profits. An entrepreneur can't afford to ignore trends.

But book writing isn't the exact same process as starting a business. Writing must be deep and unique to make an impact on readers who are smart enough to purchase and take the time to read your book. They'll be able to identify the author as a phony, too.

The best books – the ones that last through history and stand the test of time – are the ones that were written out of sheer enthusiasm and choice. They're not the ones based off a Google Trend to make a quick buck.

If aspiring authors are hoping to make hundreds of thousands of dollars because of some book they write, then they should just take up a full-time job. Writing books is not a lucrative profession. It's why so many of the greatest writers of all time died broke and depressed.

Why First-Time Authors Should Stay Away From Their 'Life Stories'

People who tell me they want to write books say they want to share their "life story." I've written several books, and none have been about my life story. I could've written my life story if I wanted to, but I'm not really sure what my life story is. It could be about studying, working, failures, successes, friendships, relationships, girls, basketball, my family, or one of a hundred other topics.

Most people don't know their life stories. They're a bunch of disconnected events and experiences. Jumbled ideas don't make for good books.

I *have* shared some stories *from my life* in my books… but none of the books have been about my "life story."

Since your friends won't break it to you, I will: unless you're a public figure, nobody cares about your "life story." Very few no-name authors become bestselling celebrities because of the autobiographies they write. They were likely famous first, so they had a platform to sell their books to.

Stephen Covey and Eckart Tolle didn't write their life stories… neither did Darwin, Machiavelli, or Freud. They instead took instances from their life to tell stories greater than themselves.

Tucker Max's first books were about his life, but he only focused on writing about his sexual escapades during his mid and late-20s. He didn't waste words on how he felt being fired from his jobs or having shitty parents.

Every chapter of his early books is focused on sex and women. Whether you like the subject matter or not, his books have gone on to sell millions of copies, and he is one of three authors (the other two are Michael Lewis and Malcolm Gladwell) to have three *New York Times* bestselling books **at the same time**.

Maya Angelou, Malcolm X and Stephen King wrote their life stories in autobiographies. The books are classics. They are critically acclaimed.

But you're not Maya Angelou, Malcolm X, or Stephen King. Once you get to their level, you can publish your life story.

Until then, focus on what you're good at. That's where you need to start.

Fiction writing is different though. If you want to write about your "life story" in a fictionalized context, then by all means, go ahead. Fiction writing is about literary skill, talent and thematic elements. If you nail these down, then your book can do very well… even if you're a no-name author.

But remember… J.K. Rowling and E.L. James didn't write their life stories when they were getting started.

Chapter 4
4 WAYS TO PREPARE TO WRITE

Writing is a skill that takes years to master. Some of the smartest and most qualified people I know are lousy writers. Unqualified people (folks without college degrees, for example) are even more atrocious in their writing abilities.

I've met so many people who can barely write or speak properly. It's astounding how some people I've previously worked with continue to stay employed despite their lack of aptitude. To external partners, colleagues, and clients, these people come across as illiterate.

I've hired freelancers for my businesses, and it still surprises me how difficult it is to find good writers who write from the heart, show command of the English language, and understand grammar and mechanics.

Writing effectively takes talent, smarts, effort, and practice. It's not enough to be good in one of these areas. Some people just aren't born to be writers... just like some people aren't born to be athletes or entrepreneurs.

People judge you based on how well you write, speak, and present yourself. If you can master each of these things, then you will always find yourself in favorable positions as an authority figure and respected individual.

Here are some tips that have helped me become a better writer:

1) **Understand grammar**

   I loved grammar classes during elementary and middle school. Surprisingly, most public and private schools don't teach grammar anymore. This is a shame.

   Learning the rules of grammar is the first step to writing effectively. Many people think grammar is useless, but if you don't have the ability to even write a basic paragraph, then writing anything at all becomes very difficult.

2) **Read your favorite writers to develop and hone your own writing style**

   I hated to read as a child. It wasn't until the end of high school that I developed a passion for reading books. Now, I read for a minimum of five hours every week: books, blogs, newsletters, and more.

   Reading good writing fosters good writing… but not all great writing will resonate with you. For example, I don't understand Shakespeare or Walt

Whitman… but I could read Malcolm Gladwell, Michael Lewis, or Tucker Max for the rest of my life and be happy and entertained.

3) **Dig down to find yourself**

Most people are running away from themselves. They refuse to acknowledge who they are.

Good writers are the opposite. They go deep into their souls and analyze themselves more than the average person. That's why so many great writers were suicidal, depressed, or alcoholic.

4) **Unleash yourself**

The best writers are the ones who hold nothing back. They aren't afraid of what the public will think about their thoughts or ideas. They let their mind do the writing, not their fingers.

If you want to be creative and unique, just let it all out.

Chapter 5
HOW TO WRITE IF YOU'RE NOT A WRITER

After deciding the topic for your book, someone needs to write. There are several strategies to do this.

I love to write, so I prefer to write everything myself. I want to come across as genuine, and I also want my efforts to show in all elements of the book.

People who don't like or don't have time to write can still publish books to get their names out there and build their brands and clientele. If you fall into this category, then here's what you should do:

Get transcribers to ask you questions. The transcribers can transcribe your answers. Then, you can send the transcription to an editor, who would make the sentences and paragraphs flow logically. Although this could cost five-figures if done with high quality, it is quick and efficient for businesses or people who don't have time but have money to spend. But again, I personally like to have control over what I write and how I say things. I like to get things started on paper. An editor can then edit my stuff to improve my writing and ideas.

Alternatively, you can use a transcription software to record yourself talking in front of your computer or smartphone. Here are some I'd recommend. They all come with free versions or free trials:

Otter app – www.otter.ai
http://www.nch.com.au/scribe/
https://www.audiotranskription.de/english
https://www.inqscribe.com/
www.rev.com (provides transcription services)

Once you transcribe everything you need, then you can outsource the editing to turn your transcriptions into a book.

This is probably the easiest way to write a book with minimal effort.

If you can't write, or if you don't like to write, then don't force yourself to do it. It takes a bit of passion to write even the simplest of sentences.

Writing and publishing a book can be a brutal process. As a published author, I've spent countless months banging my head against my desk.

But at the end of it all, it'll be worth it.

The key takeaway of this chapter and this entire book is: If you want to write a book, you have to find a way to write it.

Don't waste your time on outlines and proposals. You won't execute on half the ideas you put in there that big or traditional publishers ask for. I know people who've spent months on these and never even got *started* actually *writing* their books.

Just start writing your book as if you're going to publish it yourself!

Chapter 6
WHY AUTHORS SHOULD SHARE THEIR DEEPEST SECRETS

Writing is scary... not because it's hard, but because, as a writer, you're letting the world into your inner world. You're sharing your thoughts, ideas, personality, and insecurities with everyone. Anyone can get access to this information.

The best writing is not banal, politically correct or neutral. That's boring writing.

So, don't be afraid to share your full insights and secrets. Don't be afraid to make people laugh, cry, cringe, or nod their heads. Only be afraid of making them bored.

Many writers are afraid of giving away too much information, like personal issues, ideas and secrets... but you'll be surprised at how rare it is for readers to *steal* your ideas or screw you in any way. The worst-case scenario is that someone writes a bad review about you on their blog or Amazon. If or when that happens, then you did something right.

In my experience, I've gotten way more opportunities giving away my ideas than I have infringement cases. I haven't gone after anyone for plagiarizing my thoughts to date. Just as a parent is the only person who can parent his/her child, generally, so too the parent of an idea is the only person who can parent his/her idea.

Chapter 7
THE 5 MOST IMPORTANT ELEMENTS OF 21st CENTURY BOOK PUBLISHING

The stigma around self-publishing is rapidly decreasing because readers now can't tell the difference between a professionally self-published book and a traditionally published book.

That's why 21st century book publishing is not a battle between traditional publishers vs. self-publishers. It's instead the difference between professionally published books vs. unprofessionally published books.

If a book looks unprofessional and has a bunch of grammar and spelling errors, then it doesn't matter how great the title is or how the front cover looks. People will stop reading as soon as they spot amateurism.

The traditional big publishers will always professionally publish a book. They have the infrastructure and capital to put out well-designed, fluidly-edited books. They wouldn't invest in an author of book if they weren't going to put 100% of their process into the product.

But now, self-publishers can accomplish the same and beat the traditional publishers at their own game.

The tools are available to hire good designers and editors – through channels like Fiverr and Upwork. This book lays out all the tools you need so you can write, publish and market your book *yourself*.

1) **Cover design** – People still judge books by their front covers. It's only human nature to do so.

2) **Formatting** – The covers and manuscript must be formatted professionally. I prefer 5x8 paperback interiors. They are smaller and easier to carry around.

3) **Editor** – Behind every great writer is an even better editor. Good editors don't come cheap. You'll want to find someone who can do more than just proofread for spelling, grammar and punctuation. Good editors will make technical language simple to follow. This is important because most readers are just getting to know you or the subject you're discussing. Good editors will also create attention-grabbing titles, add witty ledes/introductions to hook people, amend the manuscript so that the writing, structure and sequencing makes sense in the body, and do anything else to make the writing stronger and more appealing to the masses.

4) **Social proof** – Get experts and respected individuals in your field to write blurbs and testimonials. You can paste their testimonials on the back cover and also include a "Praise for…" page at the beginning of the manuscript. *Bowker* found that nearly a million books were self-published in 2017. Authors need to differentiate their books from the crowd, and social proof, blurbs, and testimonials do that. They mean that someone big or famous read your book and liked it. That's a big deal.

5) **Foreword** – You want your most famous supporter in your field to write a foreword to your book. Chances are, this individual has written bestselling books in the past, so by writing the foreword to your book, you can include his or her name on your front cover. This endorsement will add tremendous credibility to your work.

Chapter 8
HOW TO DESIGN & FORMAT YOUR BOOK

People still judge books by their front covers. It's only human nature to do so.

After your book's manuscript is complete, go to www.upwork.com or www.fiverr.com to find contractors who will design your front, back and spine covers.

The people you hire (even my firm) are like robots, so you'll want to ensure that you provide ample instructions on what you'd like. Lay out exactly what you want printed, provide any images, colors, and fonts you'd like, and ask for raw files and .jpg images in the following sizes:

2400x2400 (ACX/Audible Audiobook)
2820x4500 (Kindle)

These two sizes will be enough for any subsequent submissions for display or printing or postings on social media.

To submit your paperback for printing on Kindle Direct Publishing (KDP), it's necessary that you provide a PDF that includes the front cover, back cover and spine as one image. You may not understand what this means, which is why I don't recommend you try doing any of this stuff by yourself. You'll spend weeks on it. Hiring my firm or someone on a freelance site will take a few business days to do and everything will be done correctly.

Coming up is an example of what most experienced book designers require authors to submit if they'd like book design work done. I'm including the raw instructions from one of my previous books <u>FIFTY SHADES OF MARKETING: Whip Your Business Into Shape & Dominate Your Competition</u>. You can copy and paste the below as a template for what you submit to your book designer:

[EXAMPLE OF SUBMISSION FOR FULL BOOK DESIGN]

Everything must be in a single PDF that includes the front cover, back cover and spine as one image.

Please also send front cover jpg in the following sizes:
2400x2400
2820x4500

In summary, I'll need:

1) PDF of front, back and spine

2) JPG images of front cover

Front Cover

COLORS: You can pick the colors based on the image you use and the sample front cover (shown below)

SAMPLE IMAGES:

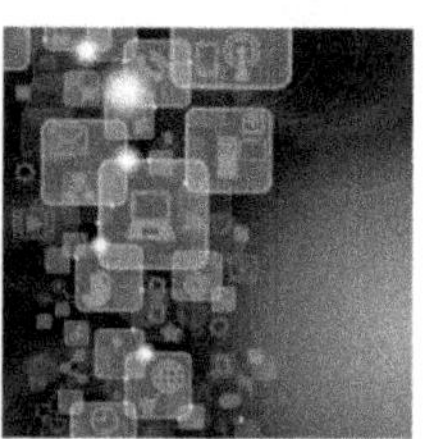

SAMPLE COVER:

From Nobody To Best Selling Author!

TEXT ON COVER (MUST INCLUDE ALL TEXT):

FIFTY SHADES OF MARKETING

Whip Your Business Into Shape & Dominate Your Competition

Naresh Vissa

Bestselling Author Of <u>PODCASTNOMICS</u>

FOREWORD BY:

Philip Kotler

Back Cover

"The 21st century strategies and principles in <u>Fifty Shades Of Marketing</u> can take any person or business to the next level."
–Jill Lublin, Bestselling Author, Global Speaker & Radical Influence Expert

The Internet has become a necessity to conduct business. Billions of people around the world are now more connected than ever before.

Whether you're an operating business or a college or job applicant, decision-makers need to know about you... what you offer... why you're awesome. Traditional marketing no longer cuts it today.

<u>Fifty Shades Of Marketing</u> lays out specific ideas, step-by-step techniques, and beneficial resources to remove the chains holding you back from success in a digital age.

"<u>Fifty Shades Of Marketing</u> is a gold mine of marketing know-how… a must read for anyone considering starting their own business. For experienced entrepreneurs, it's a refresher course on how to maximize your brand and your profits."
–Sandy Franks, Founder & CEO of the Women's Financial Alliance

Naresh Vissa has worked with leading publishers, media firms and financial institutions to improve their bottom lines through marketing. He is the Founder and CEO of Krish Media & Marketing – a full service online and digital media and marketing agency – and the author of the bestselling book, <u>PODCASTNOMICS: The Book Of Podcasting… To Make You Millions</u>.

Vissa has been featured on *USA Today*, Yahoo!, Bloomberg, MSNBC, *Huffington Post*, *Business Week*, *MSN Money*, *Business Insider*, *India Today*, *Hindustan Times* and other domestic and international media outlets.

A Krish Publishing Book
www.krishmediamarketing.com

SPINE (MAKE SURE BACKGROUND COLOR BLENDS IN WITH FRONT COVER)

TOP: Krish Publishing (facing down/normal)

MIDDLE: FIFTY SHADES OF MARKETING (facing sideways left)

BOTTOM: Naresh Vissa (facing sideways left)

[END OF EXAMPLE OF SUBMISSION FOR FULL BOOK DESIGN]

I showed you the simple instructions I laid out for my designers. Here's the AMAZING cover they came up with:

Formatting

Your book needs to be formatted for each of its versions. You'll want your book to be available in paperback, Kindle (e-book), and audiobook.

Don't format your book yourself. That would be a huge waste of time when you can pay someone little money to do a professional job. Go to www.upwork.com or www.fiverr.com to find contractors who will do the formatting for you.

Coming up is an example of instructions you can send to the formatters you hire. The following are bullets I sent to my formatters from my previous book <u>FIFTY SHADES OF MARKETING: Whip Your Business Into Shape & Dominate Your Competition</u>.

- 5x8 size
- Garamond font
- Standard spacing
- Dropcaps in the CHAPTERS ONLY (not foreword or resources or other outside sections)
- The header should contain the book title on one side and author name of another side: "Naresh Vissa".
- Footer shobuld contain page number
- The first page (cover page) with the title and author should be on the right half of the book.
- The "Praise" page should also be on the right

half of the book.

- The page with the ISBN (Page 3 in the document) should be on the left half of the book.

The audiobook version can be "formatted" by hiring someone to narrate the book. I don't recommend beginning or self-published authors doing their own narration of their books. You'd be better served paying in full or working out a revenue split with a professional voiceover artist on ACX than recording yourself stumbling. Just go to www.acx.com to find someone to narrate your audiobook.

Chapter 9
HOW TO PUBLISH YOUR BOOK TO MARKET

The book publishing industry has changed tremendously because of self-publishing. Amazon has overtaken traditional publishing houses and allowed anyone to become authors and deliver their works on its platform. Self-publishers can now also distribute to iTunes, iBooks and Audible.

You don't need to create relationships with printers, distributors, or shippers any more. The resources I'm about to lay out have already done that legwork for you.

You can publish your paperback through kdp.amazon.com. KDP offers Expanded Distribution to sell your paperbacks to physical bookstores in the U.S. as well as the ability to sell your paperback books on Amazon.ca, Amazon.com.au, and Amazon.mx. With these features, KDP's paperback distribution is on par with every major book publisher's distribution. KDP also offers the ability to purchase ads to promote paperbacks on Amazon and locally printed author copies in Europe.

You can publish your hardback through www.lulu.com. Click the "Create" tab, and you'll see the hardcover options.

You can publish your Kindle version through kdp.amazon.com.

You can publish your audiobook through www.acx.com. Your book first needs to be published in Kindle format before you can claim it for audio production on ACX. After you claim your book, you can create a posting that accepts narrator auditions for your audiobook. The process within ACX is easy to follow.

When pricing different formats of your book, follow these guidelines:

Price low. The lower the prices, the greater the number of   sales.
- Kindle: $2.99-4.99 (depending on quality and length)… must end in $Z.95 or $Z.99

- Paperback: The cheapest Kindle Direct Publishing (KDP) or Lulu allow you to sell it for… must end in $X.95 or $X.99

- Hardback: The cheapest Lulu allows you to sell it for… must end in $Y.95 or $Y.99

- Audiobook: ACX determines the price

After you have all versions of your book live, then create an   Author   Central   account   at www.authorcentral.amazon.com. You can then claim all versions of your book so it's all on one Amazon page.

You can also control how you'd like your book to be presented to searchers or visitors.

That's all you need to know. The services are simple to use and self-explanatory. I've laid out tips and tricks on preparing to use these sites throughout this book.

Chapter 10
16 WAYS TO MARKET YOUR BOOK

E-books have now become very effective forms of content marketing… if they are written and published correctly. Audiobooks and paperbacks are effective too.

Making your book available in different formats increases the chances of people finding your book… because each format will be distributed through its own unique channels.

For example, paperbacks will be distributed through Amazon, Barnes & Noble, and all their individual merchants. Audiobooks will be distributed through Amazon, Audible, iTunes, and all their individual merchants.

The more places your book is, the greater the sales. That should be the fundamental philosophy behind marketing your book… by simply getting it out there.

Here are a few more marketing tactics that have helped me publish multiple #1 bestsellers:

1. Make your **Kindle e-book available on Pre-order**. Pre-order sales can help a book hit various bestseller lists, since many retailers count all pre-orders as launch day sales. They also help build buzz and momentum, which can help lead to word-of-mouth sales later.

2. When I published one of my previous #1 bestselling book <u>PODCASTNOMICS,</u> I ran test campaigns **to give my book away for free for a limited period of time. I also ran discounted promotions** at $0.99 cents for a limited time on the Kindle e-book version to sell the book.

3. The easiest way to run discounted or free price promotions on Amazon is to join KDP Select. KeyBanc capital markets found that nearly 70% of U.S. households use Amazon Prime, which allows subscribers to "borrow" one Kindle book every month for free. The catch: they can only borrow books that are a part of the KDP Select library. When self-published authors enroll in KDP Select, their books are automatically included in this library. Borrowed books are equivalent to bought books. As more users join Amazon Prime, more books will be "borrowed" by readers. Note that once you enroll in KDP Select, you cannot submit your books to Amazon competitors (i.e. Smashwords, iBooks, your website), which is fine. Amazon is the largest book marketplace in the world, and it's only getting bigger.

4. DO NOT FREQUENTLY GIVE AWAY FREE BOOKS ON AMAZON. Free books on

Amazon carry little value to consumers. Pricing an e-book or Kindle at $2.99 is more effective than giving it away for free. Putting a price tag on something builds its value.

5. Price low. The lower the prices, the greater the number of sales. Kindle: $2.99-4.99 (depending on quality and length)… must end in $Z.95 or $Z.99

Paperback: The cheapest Kindle Direct Publishing (KDP) or Lulu allow you to sell it for… must end in $X.95 or $X.99

Hardback: The cheapest Lulu allows you to sell it for… must end in $Y.95 or $Y.99

Audiobook: ACX determines the price

6. If you have a following, then encourage your fans to write reviews on Amazon. Offer a digital version (Kindle or audiobook) of your book free of charge to your friends and family in return for reviews. You don't have to force them to right five-star reviews, but if you encourage your supporters to write reviews, there's a good chance they'll be writing five-star reviews anyway.

7. Post about your book on all your social media. This will help with 6 above.

8. Amazon gives people and products tremendous credibility. I have seen what iTunes can do to a podcast's listenership and revenue. Amazon can have the same impact on a brand-new segment – a digitally oriented, more qualified segment – you may not be penetrating. These NEW people will *find you*.

9. I use keywords in my titles to target readers. Include as many keywords as you can fit in the title and subtitle of your book. This will give potential readers a clear focus on what your book is about. It will also get search engines (including Amazon, Audible and iTunes) to list your book high in search results and suggest it as a related book to other books in its categories based on words in the title.

10. I also advertised on and rented e-mail lists (more about this in the next chapter).

11. I sent sales e-mails to my mailing list. It's taken me years to build up my mailing list, but every time I'm out with a new book, I keep my file updated and offer special promotions/discounts to help drive sales. If you want to get on my FREE mailing list/newsletter, then visit www.nareshvissa.com.

12. Reddit AMAs ("Ask Me Anything") are platforms for unique individuals to answer questions about anything. Celebrities give AMAs every day, but even little guys like me can have what are called IAmA (I am a...). **When I released my book PODCASTNOMICS, I hosted an IAmA** (IAmA Author of PODCASTNOMICS and have Generated Millions Of Dollars Through Podcasting. AMA!), and the focus was on podcasting. Complete strangers asked me anything from how to start a podcast to how to make money from podcasts. The AMA ended up generating book sales for me, and it's still on the Reddit forum archives, so anyone can find it years after it took place. To do an IAmA or a version of an AMA, sign up for a free username to Reddit and then Google, "Reddit IAmA." Click the first site that pops up, and then you'll find instructions on the right sidebar of Reddit to get started.

13. Include one testimonial snippet from a big-name expert on the front cover and two or three testimonials from experts on the back cover. This adds mainstream credibility. As much as you shouldn't judge a book by its front cover, the fact of the matter is that it's only human nature to do so.

14. Make a "free sample," like the entire first chapter, readily viewable online or downloadable free of charge. This will be a great opportunity to plug your websites, products, and anything else that can improve lead-generation, since the "free sample" of your book will display them.

15. Be a guest on podcasts that are published on iTunes. Here's why… podcasts will be on iTunes forever. They have a pass-along effect and long shelf life. A century from now, the mp3s will still be available for download. iTunes has crossed more than two billion podcast downloads, and that number is growing rapidly. There are also now more than 300,000 podcasts on iTunes too. With so many podcasts come great opportunities for interviews with authors like you. Now, think about the types of people who own Apple products… we're talking about folks who have some tech savvy and money to spend. The moment a user "Subscribes" to a podcast on iTunes, they have committed to receive all of a podcast's episodes indefinitely. This means they actually *want* to listen to every show. And it means this user is highly qualified. They're likely educated, working-class or studying, and have money to spend to improve themselves. THIS IS THE ULTIMATE LEAD. NO OTHER MARKETING CHANNEL WILL PROVIDE HIGHER QUALITY LEADS. In essence, Apple already does the filtering for podcasters. So, as a guest on a podcast, you'll be exposed to a very qualified audience. Being a guest on a podcast with 1,000 listeners is equivalent to giving a speech to 1,000 attendees in a private auditorium. Consequently, it's not just hosts who stand to benefit from podcasting. Guests on podcasts have a great opportunity to sell themselves and their products too.

Podcasts are always looking for authors who are experts in niche areas. For authors, the podcast tour has replaced the book tour. It's no longer necessary to travel around the world to meet readers and autograph books. Authors can instead hold webinars or do a bunch of podcast interviews to get the word out and then forward folks to Amazon to buy their books… from their home and in their pajamas! To find podcasts to pitch yourself on, open the Podcasts app on your iOS device or the Podcasts section in iTunes, and search your expertise. For example, if your niche is digital art, then type in "digital art" or "painting." If your niche is "stripping," then type in "stripping." See what pops up. If there are podcast shows in your niche, then contact those shows and pitch yourself. You can get the website of the show through its iTunes page. If it's not provided, then Google the show or the name of the host to find contact info. *Note: BlogTalkRadio is a competitor to iTunes and has many shows too. The quality of listeners and return on BlogTalkRadio is not as strong though. You can apply the same principles I laid out on getting iTunes podcast interviews to BlogTalkRadio.*

16. Keep writing and publishing new books. Coming out with books will help you garner a wider audience that will be interested in your other books. I've published four books to date, and they all help market each other.

The writing process, from beginning to end, can take years. The publishing and marketing process, from beginning to end, can take up to six months.

To fully self-publish and market, it costs a minimum of about $300 per book (not including time).

But the results have been worthwhile for me. I've gotten many new clients and partnership deals thanks to my books… and I've gotten these deals because of the successful marketing behind my books.

Chapter 11
HOW RENTING A MAILING LIST HELPED ME BECOME A #1 BESTSELLER

When I released my book <u>PODCASTNOMICS: The Book Of Podcasting… To Make You Millions</u>, I was disappointed with initial sales. I did a couple of Reddit AMAs, was interviewed by some small print and broadcast media, and used social media to spread the word. My book still couldn't crack 100 books sold.

Fortunately, I found a targeted blog geared towards podcasters, contacted the administrator, and asked him if I could advertise to his mailing list for nearly $300. He said very few people contacted him to advertise and that he never even thought of accepting advertising.

He agreed to my request and sent an e-mail out on my behalf to his list. He teased my book and recommended it as required reading for all podcasters.

Within 24 hours, I sold more than 90 copies of the book, and later that week, it climbed all the way to #1 in its primary category on Amazon's bestseller list. I recouped my advertising expense with that one quick and simple send.

And because it rose the charts, Amazon then started pushing my book out because they thought it would sell well moving forward… and it has. The book has gone on to sell more than 10,000 copies over its first four years in circulation.

RESOURCES

I laid out a lot of material in the book. It's impossible to remember everything… so I'll lay out the "smaller picture" resources you can use.

These resources are websites, apps, products and services to help you write, publish and market your book. They are not big picture tools like Facebook, Instagram, and WordPress. Those resources are referenced throughout the book.

Outsourcing Tasks (formatting, book cover, design, editing, etc.)

www.fiverr.com

www.upwork.com

Transcribing

Otter app – www.otter.ai

www.nch.com.au/scribe

www.audiotranskription.de/english

www.inqscribe.com

www.rev.com

Self-Publishing Books

www.lulu.com – Publish a **hardback** to Amazon.

kdp.amazon.com – Publish a **Kindle e-book** to Amazon or **paperback** to Amazon, BarnesAndNoble.com, and many other online and physical retailers. KDP offers Expanded Distribution to sell your paperbacks to physical bookstores in the U.S. as well as the ability to sell your paperback books on Amazon.ca, Amazon.com.au, and Amazon.mx. With these features, KDP's paperback distribution is on par with every major book publisher's distribution. KDP also offers the ability to purchase ads to promote paperbacks on Amazon and locally printed author copies in Europe.

www.acx.com – Find someone to narrate your audiobook and then publish it to Amazon and iTunes.

www.smashwords.com – Publish e-books to iBooks. Note that once you enroll in KDP Select, you cannot submit your books to Amazon competitors (i.e. Smashwords, iBooks, your website), which is fine. Amazon is the largest book marketplace in the world, and it's only getting bigger.

www.authorcentral.amazon.com – Use after you have all versions of your book live.

PR

<u>THE NEW PR: 21st Century Public Relations Strategies & Resources... To Reach Millions</u> by Naresh Vissa

Reddit IAmA – www.reddit.com/r/IAmA

www.helpareporter.com – Become a source by getting expert requests from media and journalists delivered straight to your e-mail inbox.

www.RadioGuestList.com – Similar to *Help A Reporter Out*, *Radio Guest List* only sends out radio and podcast queries.

www.krishmediamarketing.com

Marketing Books

<u>FIFTY SHADES OF MARKETING: Whip Your Business Into Shape & Dominate Your Competition</u> by Naresh Vissa

THE NEW PR: 21st Century Public Relations Strategies & Resources... To Reach Millions by Naresh Vissa

If you need any online/digital marketing or publishing services performed, then e-mail me at Naresh at KrishMediaMarketing.com and my firm, Krish Media & Marketing, should have solutions for you. I'm also glad to answer any questions you have

to point you in the right direction.

STAY IN TOUCH

Tweet me @xnareshx.

Visit www.nareshvissa.com_to subscribe to my FREE newsletter mailing list.

For a full list of services my marketing and publishing firm Krish Publishing offers, visit www.krishmediamarketing.com.

If you have any questions or would like my publishing company, Krish Publishing, to consult or publish your book, e-mail me at naresh at krishmediamarketing dot com.

Please leave a review of this book on Amazon!

REFERENCES

Bercovici, J. Amazon Vs. Book Publishers, By The Numbers. 12 February 2014, https://www.forbes.com/sites/jeffbercovici/2014/02/10/amazon-vs-book-publishers-by-the-numbers/#ffed7f84ef9d

Bosman, Julie, and Michael J. de la Merced. "Borders Files for Bankruptcy." *The New York Times*, The New York Times, 16 Feb. 2011, www.dealbook.nytimes.com/2011/02/16/borders-files-for-bankruptcy/?_r=0.

Coker, M. Smashwords., 23 December 2015, http://blog.smashwords.com/2015/12/2016-book-publishing-predictions.html.

Helmore, Edward. "Barnes & Noble: Why It Could Soon Be the Bookshop's Final Chapter." *The Guardian*, Guardian News and Media, 12 May 2018, www.theguardian.com/books/2018/may/12/barnes-noble-bookstores-retail-amazon.

Press, G. Inventing The Telephone, The Mechanical Automation Of Work, And Searching By Associative Links. *Forbes*, 05 March 2017. https://www.forbes.com/sites/gilpress/2017/03/05/inventing-the-telephone-the-mechanical-automation-of-work-and-searching-by-associative-links/#3b8b037a2a91.

ProQuest. (n.d.). News 2017 - Self-Publishing ISBNs Climbed 8% Between 2015-2016. http://www.bowker.com/news/2017/Self-Publishing-ISBNs-Climbed-8-Between-2015-2016.html.

Ravikant, Kamal. Love yourself like your life depends on it. United States: K. Ravikant, 2012.

Rexaline, S. "Survey: Two-Thirds Of US Households Have Amazon Prime Memberships (NASDAQ:AMZN)". Benzinga, 12 April 2018. https://www.benzinga.com/analyst-ratings/analyst-color/18/04/11497368/keybanc-survey-two-thirds-of-us-households-have-amazon-

Vissa, Naresh. *Fifty Shades of Marketing: Whip Your Business into Shape & Dominate Your Competition*. Krish Publishing, 2015.

Vissa, Naresh. *Podcastnomics: the Book of Podcasting ... to Make You Millions*. Krish Publishing, 2014.